Preface
(for parents)

The Holy Quran is a very special book that was revealed to the
Holy Prophet Muhammad *(peace be upon him)* by **Allah** *(swt)*

'The Holy Quran Made Easy For Kids: Volume 1, Surah 11-20' are here to help you and your child (5+ years) on the journey of understanding the Holy Quran together, as well as assist in the progression of understanding Islam.

Do remember this book is not a translation, it is adapted text from a from a range of Ayat in the Holy Quran which have been selected for a younger audience.

As these books have many words (ayahs and verses) that are included in the Holy Quran, all of which are special, **we ask that you treat not only this book, but all other copies of religious text with respect.**

Do make sure that you do not leave your books where they could get damaged or in places they are not supposed to be.

Have plenty of fun with these wonderful collections and we hope In'sha'Allah your child has the best start in life when it comes to their faith.

© Copyright 2019 Safoo Publications

Written by Amal Al-Aride

Illustrated by Kasim Al-Janabi

All rights reserved. Without limiting the rights under the copyright reserved above, no part of this publication may be reproduced, stored in, or introduced into a retrieval system, or transmitted in any form or by any means (electronic, mechanical, photocopying, recording, or otherwise) without prior written permission.

THE HOLY QURAN

Made Easy for Kids
Vol. 1, Surah 11-20

This is the Book (the Quran), whereof there is no doubt, a guidance to those who are Al-Muttaqoon (the pious and righteous persons who fear Allah much (abstain from all kinds of sins and evil deeds which He has forbidden) and love Allah much (perform all kinds of good deeds which He has ordained)).

Quran (Surah Al-Baqarah, Verse 2)

The Holy Quran is a book which is truthful and honest, it's a gift for those who are good, who love Allah (swt), do not do bad things and do that which Allah asks.

Surah Hud
Ayah 40-41
Prophet Hud

Allah *Subhana wata'alah* *The Amazing!* sent down water that overfilled the earth, he told **Prophet Nuh** (Peace be upon him) to build a ship and make sure that on board there were two (a male and female) of every animal.

All the people who were good at the time like his family and friends were **on board** too,

and with a **Bismillah** Prophet Nuh sailed to find land with the help of Allah, who is the most **loving and kind.**

> This Surah is named after Prophet Hud (pbuh) If you read this Surah on Fridays Allah will send you to heaven with all the other Prophets.

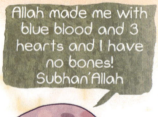

> Allah made me with blue blood and 3 hearts and I have no bones! Subhan'Allah

بِسْمِ اللهِ الرَّحْمٰنِ الرَّحِيْمِ

In the name of Allah, the infinitely Compassionate and Merciful.

حَتّىٰ إِذَا

Until, when

جَآءَ أَمْرُنَا وَفَارَ التَّنُّوْرُ قُلْنَا احْمِلْ فِيْهَا مِنْ

Our command came, and the volcano erupted, We said,

كُلٍّ زَوْجَيْنِ اثْنَيْنِ وَ أَهْلَكَ إِلَّا مَنْ سَبَقَ عَلَيْهِ

"Board into it a pair of every kind, and your family, except those against whom

الْقَوْلُ وَمَنْ اٰمَنَ ۚ وَمَآ اٰمَنَ مَعَهٗۤ إِلَّا قَلِيْلٌ ۝

the sentence has already been passed and those who have believed." But those who believed with him were only a few.

وَقَالَ ارْكَبُوْا فِيْهَا بِسْمِ اللهِ مَجْرٰىهَا وَمُرْسٰىهَا ۚ

He said, "Embark in it. In the name of Allah shall be its sailing and its anchorage.

إِنَّ رَبِّيْ لَغَفُوْرٌ رَّحِيْمٌ ۝

My Lord is indeed Forgiving and Merciful."

HOLY QURAN 11:40-41

بِسْمِ اللَّهِ الرَّحْمَٰنِ الرَّحِيمِ

Surah Yusuf
Ayah 2-5
Yusuf

Allah *Subhana wata'alah — The Amazing!* sent the Holy Quran in Arabic so that people could understand it.

It has the best **true** stories and there's lots of things it teaches you. Like the story of Prophet Yusuf (Peace be upon him), he was so good that he had a dream about the **stars, sun** and **the moon** bowing towards him.

When he told his father **Prophet Yaqub** (Peace be upon him) who was also good and knew lots about what dreams meant, he told Prophet Yusuf not to say a word because if anyone knew Iblees could tempt his brothers into hurting him.

Iblees is terrible, he makes people do bad things and he doesn't like anyone.

Prophet Yusuf (pbuh) was much smaller than his brothers, they were meant to look after him but instead they threw him down a well! Allah always kept him safe and if you read this surah Allah wil keep you safe too.

بِسْمِ اللهِ الرَّحْمٰنِ الرَّحِيْمِ

In the name of Allah, the infinitely Compassionate and Merciful.

اِنَّآ اَنْزَلْنٰهُ
We have revealed

قُرْاٰنًا عَرَبِيًّا لَّعَلَّكُمْ تَعْقِلُوْنَ ۞ نَحْنُ نَقُصُّ
it an Arabic Quran, so that you may understand. We narrate to you

عَلَيْكَ اَحْسَنَ الْقَصَصِ بِمَآ اَوْحَيْنَآ اِلَيْكَ هٰذَا
the most accurate history, by revealing to you this Quran,

الْقُرْاٰنَ ۖ وَاِنْ كُنْتَ مِنْ قَبْلِهٖ لَمِنَ الْغٰفِلِيْنَ ۞
Although, prior to it, you were of the unaware.

اِذْ قَالَ يُوْسُفُ لِاَبِيْهِ يٰٓاَبَتِ اِنِّيْ رَاَيْتُ اَحَدَ عَشَرَ
When Joseph said to his father, "O my father, I saw eleven planets,

كَوْكَبًا وَّالشَّمْسَ وَالْقَمَرَ رَاَيْتُهُمْ لِيْ سٰجِدِيْنَ ۞
and the sun, and the moon; I saw them bowing down to me."

قَالَ يٰبُنَيَّ لَا تَقْصُصْ رُءْيَاكَ عَلٰٓى اِخْوَتِكَ
He said, "O my son, do not relate your vision to your brothers,

فَيَكِيْدُوْا لَكَ كَيْدًا ۗ اِنَّ الشَّيْطٰنَ لِلْاِنْسَانِ عَدُوٌّ
lest they plot and scheme against you. Satan is man's sworn

مُّبِيْنٌ ۞
enemy.

HOLY QURAN 12: 2-5

Surah Ar-Ra'd
Ayah 16-17
The Thunder

Allah made heaven and earth, there is only **one of Allah**.

Subhana wata'alah
The Amazing!

He has no mother nor does He have sons. He can make anything and has created **everything**, nothing is as great as He is. Allah is the one who makes it rain, the one who makes the rivers **flow** and inside the middle of the earth Allah has placed fire and heat to make metals and **gold**.

If you read this Surah often you will get lots of reward and be one of the precious ones in heaven

The **wonders** of the world is how Allah shows us that **he is** amazing as He made everything so **perfect**.

Allah made the earth's core super hot and this is where lots of precious metals are found, like me!

بِسْمِ اللَّهِ الرَّحْمَٰنِ الرَّحِيمِ

In the name of Allah, the infinitely Compassionate and Merciful.

قُلْ مَن رَّبُّ

Say, "Who is the Lord

السَّمَاوَاتِ وَالْأَرْضِ ۚ قُلِ اللَّهُ ۚ قُلْ أَفَاتَّخَذْتُم مِّن

of the heavens and the earth?" Say, "Allah." Say, "

دُونِهِ أَوْلِيَاءَ لَا يَمْلِكُونَ لِأَنفُسِهِمْ نَفْعًا وَلَا ضَرًّا ۚ

Have you taken besides Him protectors, who have no power to profit

قُلْ هَلْ يَسْتَوِي الْأَعْمَىٰ وَالْبَصِيرُ أَمْ هَلْ تَسْتَوِي

or harm even themselves?" Say, "Are the blind and the seeing equal?

الظُّلُمَاتُ وَالنُّورُ ۗ أَمْ جَعَلُوا لِلَّهِ شُرَكَاءَ خَلَقُوا

Or are darkness and light equal? Or have they assigned to Allah associates,

كَخَلْقِهِ فَتَشَابَهَ الْخَلْقُ عَلَيْهِمْ ۚ قُلِ اللَّهُ خَالِقُ

who created the likes of His creation, so that the creations seemed to them alike?

كُلِّ شَيْءٍ وَهُوَ الْوَاحِدُ الْقَهَّارُ ۝ أَنزَلَ مِنَ السَّمَاءِ

Say, "Allah is the Creator of all things, and He is The One, the Irresistible."

مَاءً فَسَالَتْ أَوْدِيَةٌ بِقَدَرِهَا فَاحْتَمَلَ السَّيْلُ

He sends down water from the sky, and riverbeds flow according to their capacity.

زَبَدًا رَّابِيًا ۚ وَمِمَّا يُوقِدُونَ عَلَيْهِ فِي النَّارِ

The current carries swelling froth. And from what they heat in fire of

ابْتِغَاءَ حِلْيَةٍ أَوْ مَتَاعٍ زَبَدٌ مِّثْلُهُ ۚ كَذَٰلِكَ يَضْرِبُ

ornaments or utensils comes a similar froth. Thus Allah exemplifies truth

اللَّهُ الْحَقَّ وَالْبَاطِلَ ۚ فَأَمَّا الزَّبَدُ فَيَذْهَبُ جُفَاءً ۖ

and falsehood. As for the froth, it is swept

وَأَمَّا مَا يَنفَعُ النَّاسَ فَيَمْكُثُ فِي الْأَرْضِ ۚ كَذَٰلِكَ

away, but what benefits the people remains in the ground.

يَضْرِبُ اللَّهُ الْأَمْثَالَ ۝

Thus Allah presents the analogies.

HOLY QURAN 13:16-17

Surah Ibrahim
Ayah 22-23

Prophet Ibrahim

Iblees tells us "**Allah** (*Subhana wata'alah - The Amazing!*) always tells the **truth** and I am one of those who lie. Anyone who listens to me instead of Allah will **never** be happy. I haven't done anything wrong. I only invite you to do bad things, you're the ones who do it. So you can't blame me, it was all you. And don't ask me for help because I don't want to **help** you, I want you to get in lots of trouble so you are left with nothing".

But Allah tells us that those who do good, are **kind** and believe in Allah, they will have gardens in heaven and will always **be safe**, if they always try to avoid Iblees (by doing good things).

> I have cold blood and like warm places.

> This Surah is named after Prophet Ibrahim pbuh and he built the Kabaa.

بِسْمِ اللَّهِ الرَّحْمَٰنِ الرَّحِيمِ

In the name of Allah, the infinitely Compassionate and Merciful.

وَقَالَ الشَّيْطَانُ لَمَّا قُضِيَ

And Satan will say, when the issue is settled,

الْأَمْرُ إِنَّ اللَّهَ وَعَدَكُمْ وَعْدَ الْحَقِّ وَوَعَدتُّكُمْ

"Allah has promised you the promise of truth, and I promised you, but I failed you. I had no authority

فَأَخْلَفْتُكُمْ ۖ وَمَا كَانَ لِيَ عَلَيْكُم مِّن سُلْطَانٍ إِلَّا

over you, except that I called you, and you answered me. So do not blame me, but blame yourselves.

أَن دَعَوْتُكُمْ فَاسْتَجَبْتُمْ لِي ۖ فَلَا تَلُومُونِي وَلُومُوا

I cannot come to your aid, nor can you come to my aid.

أَنفُسَكُم ۖ مَّا أَنَا بِمُصْرِخِكُمْ وَمَا أَنتُم بِمُصْرِخِيَّ ۖ إِنِّي

I reject your associating with me in the past. The wrongdoers

كَفَرْتُ بِمَا أَشْرَكْتُمُونِ مِن قَبْلُ ۗ إِنَّ الظَّالِمِينَ

will have a torment most painful." But those who believed

لَهُمْ عَذَابٌ أَلِيمٌ ۝ وَأُدْخِلَ الَّذِينَ آمَنُوا وَعَمِلُوا

and did good deeds will be admitted into gardens beneath which rivers flow,

الصَّالِحَاتِ جَنَّاتٍ تَجْرِي مِن تَحْتِهَا الْأَنْهَارُ خَالِدِينَ

to remain therein forever, by leave of their Lord.

فِيهَا بِإِذْنِ رَبِّهِمْ ۖ تَحِيَّتُهُمْ فِيهَا سَلَامٌ ۝

Their greeting therein will be: "Peace."

HOLY QURAN 14 : 22-23

Surah Al-Hijr
Ayah 85-86
The Rock

Subhana wata'alah
The Amazing!

Allah made heaven and **earth** and all of this is **true**, soon we will all meet Allah and before that happens we should try to **forgive** those who may have done things that have upset us. We should always try to do **better** because Allah knows everything as He made **everything.**

Allah created more than 400 billion stars in our galaxy

بِسْمِ اللهِ الرَّحْمٰنِ الرَّحِيْمِ

In the name of Allah, the infinitely Compassionate and Merciful.

اِنَّ رَبَّكَ هُوَ الْخَلَّاقُ الْعَلِيْمُ ۝ وَلَقَدْ

We did not create the heavens and the earth, and what lies between them, except with truth.

اٰتَيْنٰكَ سَبْعًا مِّنَ الْمَثَانِي وَالْقُرْاٰنَ الْعَظِيْمَ ۝

The Hour is coming, so forgive with gracious forgiveness. Your Lord is the All-Knowing Creator.

HOLY QURAN 15 : 85-86

بِسْمِ اللهِ الرَّحْمٰنِ الرَّحِيْمِ

In the name of Allah, the infinitely Compassionate and Merciful.

هُوَ الَّذِيْٓ اَنْزَلَ مِنَ السَّمَآءِ

It is He Who sends down for you from the sky water,

مَآءً لَّكُمْ مِّنْهُ شَرَابٌ وَّمِنْهُ شَجَرٌ فِيْهِ تُسِيْمُوْنَ ۝

From it is drink, and with it grows vegetation for grazing.

يُنْۢبِتُ لَكُمْ بِهِ الزَّرْعَ وَالزَّيْتُوْنَ وَالنَّخِيْلَ

And He produces for you grains with it, and olives, and date-palms, and grapes,

وَالْاَعْنَابَ وَمِنْ كُلِّ الثَّمَرٰتِؕ اِنَّ فِيْ ذٰلِكَ لَاٰيَةً

and all kinds of fruits. Surely in that is a sign for people who think.

لِّقَوْمٍ يَّتَفَكَّرُوْنَ ۝ وَسَخَّرَ لَكُمُ الَّيْلَ وَالنَّهَارَ

12. And He regulated for you the night and the day; and the sun, and the moon,

وَالشَّمْسَ وَالْقَمَرَؕ وَالنُّجُوْمُ مُسَخَّرٰتٌۢ بِاَمْرِهٖؕ اِنَّ

and the stars are disposed by His command.

فِيْ ذٰلِكَ لَاٰيٰتٍ لِّقَوْمٍ يَّعْقِلُوْنَ ۝ وَمَا ذَرَاَ لَكُمْ

Surely in that are signs for people who ponder.

فِي الْاَرْضِ مُخْتَلِفًا اَلْوَانُهٗؕ اِنَّ فِيْ ذٰلِكَ لَاٰيَةً

13. And whatsoever He created for you on earth is of diverse colors. Surely in

لِّقَوْمٍ يَّذَّكَّرُوْنَ ۝

that is a sign for people who are mindful.

HOLY QURAN 16 : 10-13

Surah Al-Isra
Ayah 23-25
Children of Israel

Subhana wata'alah — The Amazing!

Allah tells us that there is only one of Him and He made all of us. Allah also tells us that we should always remember to be kind to our parents and that we should look after them when they get **older**. Allah tells us to be kind to our parents and never answer them back with bad **words**, always be **nice**. We should pray for our **parents** because they brought us up when we were **little**. Allah knows everything and we should all be good and ask for forgiveness for things that we do as Allah is the most forgiving and the kindest.

> The children of Israel in the Holy Quran, Bible and Torah are Prophet Yaqubs (pbuh) children.

بِسْمِ اللهِ الرَّحْمٰنِ الرَّحِيْمِ

In the name of Allah, the infinitely Compassionate and Merciful.

وَقَضٰى رَبُّكَ اَلَّا تَعْبُدُوْٓا اِلَّآ اِيَّاهُ وَبِالْوَالِدَيْنِ

Your Lord has commanded that you worship none but Him, and that you be good

اِحْسَانًا ۚ اِمَّا يَبْلُغَنَّ عِنْدَكَ الْكِبَرَ اَحَدُهُمَآ اَوْ كِلٰهُمَا

to your parents. If either of them or both of them reach old age with you,

فَلَا تَقُلْ لَّهُمَآ اُفٍّ وَّلَا تَنْهَرْهُمَا وَقُلْ لَّهُمَا قَوْلًا

do not say to them a word of disrespect, nor scold them, but say to them kind words.

كَرِيْمًا ۝ وَاخْفِضْ لَهُمَا جَنَاحَ الذُّلِّ مِنَ الرَّحْمَةِ

And lower to them the wing of humility, out of mercy, and say,

وَقُلْ رَّبِّ ارْحَمْهُمَا كَمَا رَبَّيٰنِيْ صَغِيْرًا ۝ رَبُّكُمْ اَعْلَمُ

"My Lord, have mercy on them, as they raised me when I was a child."

بِمَا فِيْ نُفُوْسِكُمْ ۚ اِنْ تَكُوْنُوْا صٰلِحِيْنَ فَاِنَّهٗ كَانَ

Your Lord knows best what is in your minds. If you are righteous,

لِلْاَوَّابِيْنَ غَفُوْرًا ۝

He is Forgiving to the obedient.

HOLY QURAN 17:23-25

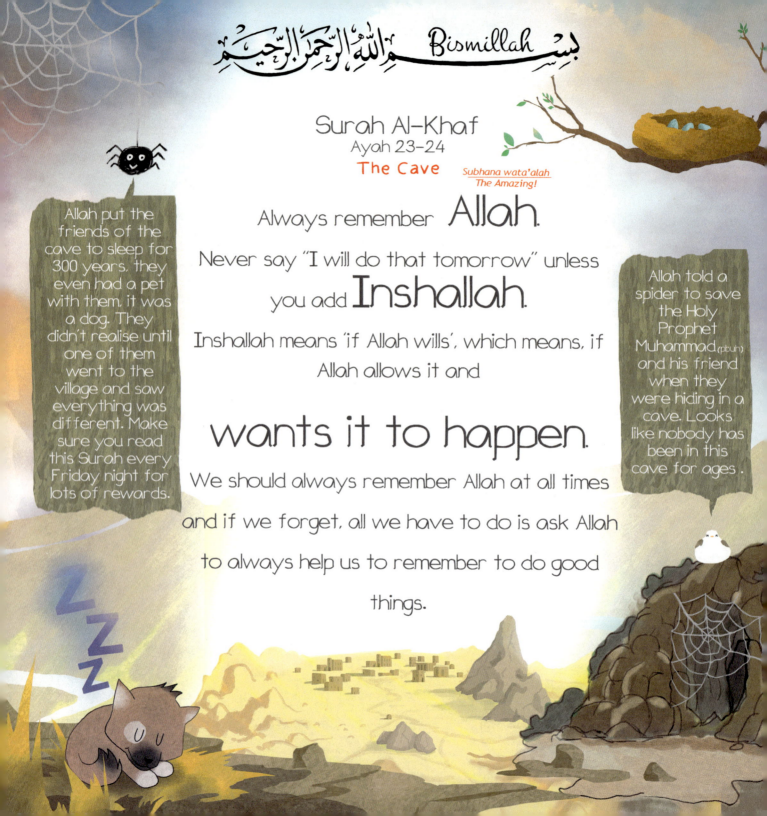

بِسْمِ اللهِ الرَّحْمٰنِ الرَّحِيْمِ

In the name of Allah, the infinitely Compassionate and Merciful.

وَلَا تَقُوْلَنَّ لِشَأْىٍ اِنِّىْ فَاعِلٌ

And never say about anything, "I will do that tomorrow."

ذٰلِكَ غَدًا ۝ اِلَّآ اَنْ يَّشَآءَ اللهُ ۚ وَاذْكُرْ رَّبَّكَ

Without saying, "If Allah wills." And remember your Lord

اِذَا نَسِيْتَ وَقُلْ عَسٰٓى اَنْ يَّهْدِيَنِ رَبِّىْ لِاَقْرَبَ

if you forget, and say, "Perhaps my Lord will guide me

مِنْ هٰذَا رَشَدًا ۝

to nearer than this in integrity."

HOLY QURAN 18 : 23-24

Surah Maryam
Ayah 34-36
Mary

Prophet **Isa** is the son of **Maryam** (Peace be upon them both), he is **honest** and good. He is a Prophet chosen by **Allah**. *Subhana wata'alah The Amazing!*

Allah does not have sons, there is only one Allah and nothing is higher than Him, when Allah wants something to happen, all He says is **"Be"** and there it is.

Prophet Jesus (peace be upon him) had said, "There is only one Allah and **I pray** to Him as that is what good people do and praying to Allah is how you become better and keep doing **good things**".

> Prophet Isa (pbuh) spoke when he was a baby! He told everyone that there was one God and that he was a prophet.

> I shouldn't really be here! I'm not in season yet! Maryam (pbuh) was so special to Allah that she was sent fruits (by Allah) that were not around at that time of year. She also has her own fruit garden in heaven because she was so amazing.

بِسْمِ اللهِ الرَّحْمٰنِ الرَّحِيْمِ

In the name of Allah, the infinitely Compassionate and Merciful.

ذٰلِكَ عِيْسَى ابْنُ مَرْيَمَ ۚ قَوْلَ الْحَقِّ

That is Jesus son of Mary—the Word of truth about which they doubt.

الَّذِيْ فِيْهِ يَمْتَرُوْنَ ۝ مَا كَانَ لِلّٰهِ اَنْ يَّتَّخِذَ مِنْ

It is not for Allah to have a child—glory be to Him.

وَّلَدٍ ۙ سُبْحٰنَهٗ ۚ اِذَا قَضٰى اَمْرًا فَاِنَّمَا يَقُوْلُ لَهٗ كُنْ

To have anything done, He says to it, "Be," and it becomes.

فَيَكُوْنُ ۝ وَاِنَّ اللهَ رَبِّيْ وَرَبُّكُمْ فَاعْبُدُوْهُ ۚ هٰذَا

"Allah is my Lord and your Lord, so worship Him.

صِرَاطٌ مُّسْتَقِيْمٌ ۝

That is a straight path."

HOLY QURAN 19:34-36

Surah TaHa
Ayah 14-16
Taha

Allah *(Subhana wata'alah — The Amazing!)* told Prophet Musa *(Peace be upon him)*

"I have chosen you Prophet Musa and you will listen to what I say.

I am Allah and there is only **one** of me, so **pray** to me everyday and always **remember me** when you pray.

Always try to do good things because you never know what the next **hour brings**, make sure you are **kind** and good for in the end you will be with those I send to **heaven**."

Allah inspired Musa's (pbuh) mother to place him in a basket and set him adrift in the Nile river to protect him.

بِسْمِ اللَّهِ الرَّحْمَٰنِ الرَّحِيمِ

In the name of Allah, the infinitely Compassionate and Merciful.

إِنَّنِي أَنَا اللَّهُ لَا إِلَٰهَ إِلَّا أَنَا

I am Allah. There is no God but I. So serve Me,

فَاعْبُدْنِي وَأَقِمِ الصَّلَاةَ لِذِكْرِي ۝ إِنَّ السَّاعَةَ آتِيَةٌ

and practice the prayer for My remembrance. The Hour is coming—

أَكَادُ أُخْفِيهَا لِتُجْزَىٰ كُلُّ نَفْسٍ بِمَا تَسْعَىٰ ۝ فَلَا

but I keep it almost hidden—so that each soul will be paid for what it endeavors.

يَصُدَّنَّكَ عَنْهَا مَنْ لَا يُؤْمِنُ بِهَا وَاتَّبَعَ هَوَاهُ فَتَرْدَىٰ ۝

And do not let him who denies it and follows his desire turn you away from it, lest you fall.

HOLY QURAN 20:14-16

THE HOLY QURAN
Made Easy for Kids
Vol. 1, Surah's 1-10
(Selected Ayahs)

Available at Amazon in paperback and on kindle versions.

safoopublications.com

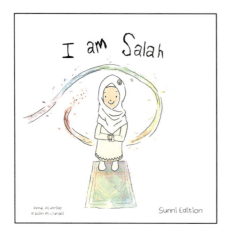 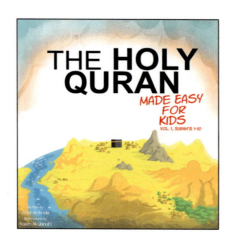 

Find more books to read at

safoopublications.com

Available at Amazon in paperback
and on kindle versions.